Susan Wood

RAPTOR BASICS...
for KIDS

Dedication

To the Creator of the magnificent birds of prey.

To Jesus, author of all living things.

Then God said, "Let the waters abound with the abundance of living creatures, and let birds fly above the earth across the face of the firmament of the heavens." So God created great sea creatures and every living thing that moves, with which the waters abounded, according to its kind, and every winged bird according to its kind. And God saw that it was good. And God blessed them ... Genesis 1:20-22

To my husband, Jonathan Wood, my inspiration ...

and my daughter, Rachel Wood, bird girl extraordinaire.

Words in Color are defined in the glossary.

FOREWORD

Attention KIDS (young and old)

How would YOU like to be able to fly through the SKY, be STRONG and FAST with eyes like binoculars and be afraid of NOTHING…?! Imagine striking FEAR into the hearts of other animals just by flying overhead!! It must be AWESOME to be a RAPTOR!

Susan Wood along with her husband Jon and daughter Rachel have lived with, studied and trained hundreds of Eagles, Hawks, Falcons and Owls for many years. Their celebration of the majesty of all Birds of Prey through their award winning "Raptor Project" shows have thrilled millions of people all around the world.

Raptor lovers rejoice! Susan Wood has opened a magical door into the private lives and wondrous world of these elusive hunters. With each paged turned Susan shines a new light on what makes these feathered predators so special. Learn how each one uses it`s formidable power and weapons to not just survive, but thrive in the tough and challenging world of the wild outdoors. As only Susan Wood can, she`s shared with us her unique insight, passion and knowledge about these special Birds.

Raptor Basics for Kids is a special book indeed! It should occupy a special place in any fledgling Bird of Prey lover's book shelf. Thank you Susan for helping us all understand and admire the wonder of Raptors!

– Floyd Scholz

World renowned Bird of Prey sculptor, author
and founder of the Vermont Raptor Academy

Contents

Photo Credits

Reinier Munguia - All photos except those mentioned below.
Jonathan Wood - Front cover, Contents, p. 1, 2, 3, 6, 14, 24,
31, 33, 35-39, 44.

Stock Photos by Depositphotos.com
Eric Isselée - p. 15, 30, 36, 43
Steve Cooper - p. 27
Steve Byland - p. 20
Stylepics - p. 3 (Egyptian Hieroglyphs)
Alexander Podshivalov - p. 12
Predrag Kostin - p. 11
Bruce MacQueen - p. 43 (nestbox)

What a thrilling sight to look up and see a majestic eagle flying high in the sky!

And while hiking through the woods we can marvel at a tiny screech owl with huge eyes sitting on a branch, staring back at us.

Eastern Screech Owl

Golden Eagle

Within the animal kingdom there is a special class of birds that are set apart from all other birds. They are the RAPTORS, hunters of the bird world, designed with special features that allow them to excel in speed, strength, hearing, eyesight, and agility.

1

Raptors are found in all parts of the world in many different habitats. Some raptors are designed for hot climates, and some for extreme cold.

Snowy Owl

Some are in cities and others live out in the country. Some raptors are even found in your own back-yard.

American Kestrel

Wherever raptors live, they must survive by catching and killing other animals. As fierce hunters, they are at the top of the food chain and rule over all other birds in the animal kingdom.

Do you know what's on a raptor's menu?

Red-tailed Hawk

Raptors have be found throughout all of history, even in ancient times. And throughout all generations, the beautiful and magnificent RAPTORS have captured the hearts of people young and old.

Falcon image carved in stone by the Egyptians.

Rachel Wood holding a Crested Caracara.

Raptors are made up of four main bird groups:

Eagles

Owls

Hawks

Falcons

4

Raptor is another name for bird of prey, and is defined as a bird that grasps and kills other animals with its feet.

Harris Hawk

Raptors are predators of the Sky

Gyrfalcon

All raptors are hunters and killers, and survive by eating other animals, even other birds. Their fierce hunting skills and features give them a very important task in nature.

There are many characteristics and traits that raptors have in common. Raptors have large, strong feet with long, sharp talons used for grasping and killing their prey.

The large, strong feet of a Golden Eagle.

They also have a strong, hooked beak for tearing the food they have caught. Raptors have no teeth, but use this sharp beak to rip up and swallow chunks of meat.

Sharp Hooked Beak

Sharp, hooked beak of a Bald Eagle

Harris Hawk

10X

All raptors have keen eyesight that is 8 to 10 times sharper than ours. As predators, their eyes are set forward in their face, giving them a fierce look.

Prey animals, such as rabbits and mice, have eyes that are set more to the side of their head, allowing them a wider field of vision to spot predators.

Both predator and prey animals have advantages, which provides a perfect balance in the wild.

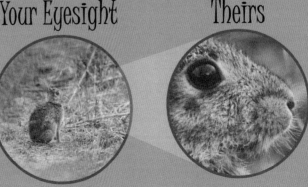

Your Eyesight   Theirs

7

Raptors are designed with speed and agility to compliment their hunting skills, which are key to their survival in the wild.

What is the fastest speed ever recorded by a raptor?

256 mph

The US Air Force named their top fighter the F-22 Raptor for its agility and speed.

Gyrfalcon

Harris hawk hunting

Each day raptors have to hunt and kill to eat and stay alive. If their hunting skills are not good, they will grow weak and will be unable to survive in the wild.

Jonathan Wood of the Raptor Project doing an educational program with GOLDEN EAGLE "Cody" who was injured from electrocution on a power line.

Many raptors with poor hunting skills or injuries are found by people and live their lives in wildlife centers. Some are used in educational programs teaching people about the important role of raptors in our world.

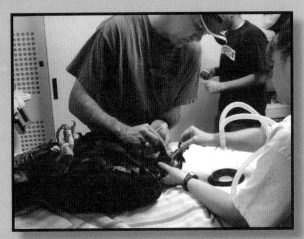

Dr. Tim Tristan working on "Cody" the Golden Eagle.

EAGLES

There are 67 species of eagles around the world, but in North America we have only two eagles, the BALD EAGLE and the GOLDEN EAGLE. These two eagles are beautiful and magnificent.

Bald Eagle

Golden Eagle

Golden Eagle

Golden Eagle

The GOLDEN EAGLE has this special name because it is brown in color with golden highlights on its feathers, especially the back of its neck. The GOLDENS hunt mostly small- and medium-sized animals, such as rabbits and ground squirrels, but they are sometimes known to hunt large animals such as deer and mountain goats, as well.

Did you know Golden Eagles can live up to 30 yeas in the wild?

Golden Eagle

A tight Squeeze!

An eagle's grip is **2000** pounds per square inch.

The females have a wingspan seven to eight feet wide and the males about six feet. Here in North America, GOLDEN EAGLES are found mostly in the western part of the United States. GOLDENS are also found in many other countries around the world.

An eagle's body has
about 7000 feathers.

Golden Eagle

13

Bald Eagle

The BALD EAGLE is our nation's symbol and looks quite handsome and patriotic alongside our beautiful American flag. BALD EAGLES have a dark brown body with a white head and tail. They were named "BALD EAGLE" from the Old English word "balde," which means "white".

Can you guess what other bird was proposed for our National symbol?

On June 20th, 1782 the Bald Eagle was adopted as the emblem of the United States of America, because of its long lifespan, strength and majestic looks. Today we can find the eagle on our currency as well as on the Great Seal of the United States of America.

Benjamin Franklin proposed the turkey as the national symbol.

The favorite food of a BALD EAGLE is fish, and they spend much of their time near lakes and streams. They will also eat land animals and will occasionally feast on a road kill.

Juvenile Bald Eagle

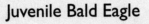

Raptors can catch & kill prey larger than themselves.

An eagle's foot is as large as a man's hand.

About fifty years ago the number of BALD EAGLES began to decline. At that time a **pesticide**, or poison called **DDT** was widely used by farmers to spray over their fields to kill bugs that were destroying the crops. The poison did kill the bugs, but those poisoned bugs were eaten by birds, animals, and eventually made it's way to raptors, who are at the top of the food chain.

Adult Bald Eagle

The DDT caused health problems for some species such as BALD EAGLES. The poison caused their eggshells to become thin and break. Many BALD EAGLES were not able to reproduce and their numbers began to drop. They were quickly put on the endangered species list and DDT was banned.

Another problem BALD EAGLES faced was that people hunted and killed these beautiful birds for their feathers and body parts. New laws were made to protect BALD EAGLES, and it is now illegal to harm eagles or ANY bird of prey. Because of these efforts, the BALD EAGLES' numbers have risen, and they are now off the endangered and threatened species list. This is one of the greatest wildlife success stories of our century.

Hawks

HAWKS are separated into two basic groups: Buteos and Accipiters. Hawks can be easily spotted and enjoyed in our every day life. Buteos, such as Red-tailed hawks, like to sit by the highways, and Accipiters, such as Cooper's hawks, love to dart through our backyards after prey. Many raptors have learned to live and thrive alongside of mankind in the world we live in.

Red-shouldered Hawk

Buteo

Cooper's Hawk

Accipiter

Buteos

Buteo hawks have large, broad wings and can be seen flying in wide circles in the air or sitting in open, visible places. The RED-TAILED HAWK is the most common buteo and is the one we see most often. They are dark brown in color with a light, creamy breast. They have a concentration of dark feathers near their belly, which is called a "belly band." Their greatest feature is their brick red tail, which is the easiest way to identify them. The juvenile birds (under one year old) have a brown tail, but will have a red tail shortly after their first molt.

All raptors go through a "molt" each year, which means that each of their feathers is pushed out and replaced by a brand new feather. This happens over a period of time, usually during the spring and summer.

Accipiters

Cooper's Hawk

Accipiter hawks are secretive birds that prefer hiding places in wooded areas. They have short wings and a long tail, which allow them to make quick turns and, stops, and to maneuver in and out of trees and bushes. An accipiter could live in a wooded area near your house, waiting patiently for a little bird to land on your deck or birdfeeder. If you have a quick eye, you may catch a flashing glimpse of this speedster as it darts in to quickly snatch its next meal, leaving only a few floating feathers behind.

Since raptors are predators, they are feared by other birds.

Osprey

Osprey

There is also a special category called fish hawk that only contains one bird, the OSPREY. The OSPREYS exclusively catch fish and are found by oceans, lakes and rivers. They scan the waters for fish that swim near the surface. Then they swoop down, splash into the water, and grab a fish with their feet, which are specially designed to grasp and hold slippery fish.

Young Ospreys

OSPREYS are larger than most hawks, but smaller than the Bald and Golden eagles. They adapt well to man-made nesting platforms, which allow people the opportunity to see them in the wild feeding and caring for their young near lakes, rivers and coastal areas.

Catfish for dinner!

Did you know? Ospreys are found in all continents except Antartica.

22

Falcons are beautiful, sleek birds with very long, pointed wings. Their bodies are designed for speed and they eat mostly birds, catching them in midair with their large, powerful feet. Falcons fly high above their prey to gain height advantage. Then they dive straight down, slicing through the air at speeds above 200 miles per hour, intersecting their prey with outstretched talons.

Gyrfalcon

Falcons

In 1986 the Aplomado falcon was listed as an endangered species. Through captive breeding programs, they are now once again nesting along the Texas gulf coast.

Falcon's Feast - Falcons prefer to eat other birds.

Aplomado Falcon

The magnificent PEREGRINE FALCON is known as the fastest animal in the world, although all of the large falcons are equally as fast.

Even the small MERLIN FALCON can dive into a flock of starlings, grabbing one with its large foot.

American Kestrel

The most common raptor in the country is actually the small, cute, and colorful AMERICAN KESTREL FALCON.

Kestrels can be seen sitting on power lines waiting for a mouse to scurry through the grass below. Although mice are its favorite food, the Kestrel also eats insects and even small birds. Often Kestrels can be seen hovering over a field before they plunge down to catch a field mouse.

Owls

Owls are beautiful and mysterious hunters of the night. They have large, round faces that are designed to collect sound, like a satellite dish. The feathers on their face grow outward from the center in a round shape called a facial disc.

Eastern Screech Owl

Great Gray Owl

The hearing of an owl is so sensitive they can detect the motion of a small mouse rustling under two feet of snow. They have been seen diving into deep snow and coming up with a mouse.

Do you know what this is?

Twelve hours after swallowing its prey, an owl spits out the bones and fur compacted as a pellet. Scientists can learn what owls eat by the contents of their pellets.

Many children dissect owl pellets as a classroom project. All birds of prey cough up a pellet to complete their digestion. The pellet is a little sack made up of fur or feathers from the animal or bird they ate. Owl pellets also contain the entire skeleton of the animal, usually a mouse, because owls don't digest the bones. Owl pellet kits are available to purchase, which contain owl pellets and charts that show pictures of skulls and bones of the typical animals that owls eat, such as mice, rats and moles.

Eurasian Eagle Owl

An owl's huge eyes give it superior vision. Not only can owls see eight to ten times sharper than we can in the daytime, they see fifty times better than we do at night. Their eyes are fixed in their sockets, which means that owls cannot move their eyes back and forth like we do.

They must turn their head to look around. Owls have so much flexibility in their necks they can turn their heads about three-fourths of the way around. Owls have twice the amount of neck bones, or vertebra, than we do. We have seven and owls have fourteen!

Barn Owl

Since most owls are nocturnal, they do most of their hunting at night. Their feathers are specially designed with soft edges, giving them silent flight. They can snatch their prey without the animal ever hearing them coming.

Owls are silent fliers, thanks to their specialized flight feathers.

Eagle Owl

Raptors have very strong legs and feet.

Some owls catch animals larger & heavier than themselves.

Great Horned Owl

Owls know how to play hide and seek.

With **camouflage** and silent flight, an owl can sneak up on its prey in the quiet of the night. Owls are hard to find in the wild because of their camouflage, which means their feathers are the same colors and patterns as the habitat they live in. A GREAT HORNED OWL is camouflaged in a tree crevice because its feathers look just like the tree trunk.

Barred Owl

Small birds often group together to attack & harass a raptor, to drive it out of the area. This is called "mobbing".

A snowy owl blends in with its artic environment with its dense, white feathers.

Snowy Owl

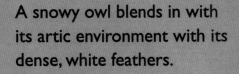

An owl can turn its head 270 degrees, almost three quarters of the way around.

Burrowing Owl

Not all owls are nocturnal. Some owls, such as the SNOWY OWL, the BURROWING OWL, the HAWK OWL and the SHORT-EARRED OWL are diurnal, hunting during the day and sleeping at night.

Although most owls hoot, some make other calls, such as the "yip" of the SHORT-EARRED OWL and the whining shrill of the BARN OWL.

Barn Owl

Short Earred Owl

RAPTOR BABIES

African Lanner Falcon in the egg.

Raptor babies hatch out of an egg.

Saker Falcon

Baby Eagle Owl

After hatching out of the egg, raptor babies are covered with soft, down feathers. Raptors are help-less when they are born and both parents take care of the young. Raptor parents tear small pieces of meat and tenderly nudge the food into the hungry mouths of their babies. Raptor babies eat the same food as their parents, only very small pieces.

Baby Eagle Owl

Baby Eagle Owl

As the raptor baby grows, adult feathers begin to appear. The adult feather pushes out and replaces the baby down feather. The baby grows very quickly and new feathers appear each day.

Harris Hawk

These raptor babies are in the middle stages of growing in their adult feathers. About half of their feathers are baby down, and half are their adult feathers. Babies cannot fly until most of their adult feathers have grown in.

Barn Owls

Burrowing Owl

Barbary Falcon

Raptors grow fast! A newly hatched eagle grows to full size in only 12 weeks. A medium size bird, such as a red-tailed hawk, grows up in 8 weeks. A small bird, like a kestrel falcon, takes only 4 weeks to be the same size as its parents.

Most full grown young birds still have some patches of down feathers here and there. But they are eagerly learning to flap their wings and fly. Even though youngsters are full size, their parents still take care of them for a few more weeks. Raptor parents take their youngsters out to show them how to hunt and kill to survive. Soon the youngsters will drift away from their parents and find their own territory to live.

Even you can help raptors!

It wasn't long ago that people thought raptors were harmful, and would try to harm or kill these magnificent birds.

But today we can help raptors by learning all we can about their lives, as well as their challenges to survive in our world.

Through education, wildlife rehabilitation, and protecting raptors, we can share our life here on earth with the most captivating birds ever created.

Young Bald Eagle being treated at the Audubon Center for Birds of Prey in Florida.

Gyrfalcon

Here are some common questions that people ask about raptors:

How often do raptors hunt?

A raptor will only hunt when it's hungry or feeding its young. For a medium-sized hawk, a meal may be made up of one squirrel or a few rodents. If the hawk only catches a small mouse, it will continue to hunt until it is full. This meal will usually last a day or two before the bird will feel hungry again. When hungry, the bird will hunt once again.

Why do birds, like red-tailed hawks, fly in circles high in the air?

Some birds like to float on air currents, or thermals, while they search for food. Their eyesight is about ten times sharper than ours. A hawk or eagle can spot a rabbit rustling in the bushes from two miles away.

Farmers often see hawks circle above as they mow the hay in their fields with their tractor. The hawks swoop down and catch rodents newly exposed by the freshly cut hay.

Can people have birds of prey as pets?

People must have wildlife licenses to have any bird of prey. Licenses must be obtained by state and federal wildlife departments as a special purpose license, such as falconry, wildlife rehabilitation, or education.

Do raptors eat bird seed, like other kinds of birds?

Raptors are carnivores and only eat meat. They cannot survive on bird seed.

Why do raptors kill and eat other animals?

Raptors are predators and are specially designed to catch and kill their prey. They play an important role in our environment because without raptors, we would be overrun by rodents, pigeons and many other animals that would eat our crops and even spread harmful diseases. Most of the time, raptors catch animals that are sick and weak, leaving a healthy balance in the environment.

If a baby bird falls from its nest, can it be put back in the nest or would the parents reject the baby?

Raptor parents, as well as other bird parents, would not reject their baby because of human touch. They will continue to feed and take care of the baby bird.

Is it possible to see owls in the daytime?

Not all owls are nocturnal. Some are diurnal, awake during the daytime. But even the nocturnal owls can sometimes be seen during the day, especially at dawn and dusk.
Just as people don't immediately sleep when it gets dark, owls can sometimes be seen awake or even hunting during the day.

Can I attract raptors to my backyard?

There are some raptors you can attract by putting up a man made wooden nest box. Kestrel falcons, screech owls, and barn owls are the most common raptor species that adapt to nest boxes. But raptors only use nest boxes for breeding and raising their young . Information on constructing nest boxes can be found online.

How long do raptors live?

Usually, the larger raptors live longer than the smaller ones. An eagle can live up to 50 years, a peregrine falcon about 25 years, and a screech owl may live 10-12 years.

Are vultures raptors?

Turkey Vulture

Although vultures are sometimes listed with raptors in many birds of prey guides and books, they are not true raptors. Raptors are hunters that kill with their feet, but vultures only eat animals that are already dead. They are the clean up crew!

Why do we see hawks perched on poles and in trees along the highways?

The grass is always nicely cut along the highways, which makes it easier for hawks to see rodents and little animals as they scurry around. They will occasionally eat a dead animal, or road kill, along the roadside.

Why do owls come out when it's dark?

Most owls are nocturnal, which means they are active at night. Owls are on the night shift. Owls are specially designed to hunt in the dark. Since most rodents are also nocturnal, there's plenty of food available for them.

Glossary

Accipiter   A type of hawk that has short wings and a long tail. In North America this group contains the sharp shinned hawk, coopers hawk and goshawk.

Birds of Prey   A bird that hunts and kills other animals for food.

Buteo   A hawk that has large, broad wings. A common buteo is a red tailed hawk.

Camouflage   A bird is camouflaged when its feathers have the same colors and patterns as its surroundings.

Captive breeding   The process of breeding animals in human controlled environments to help the species survive.

DDT   A pesticide widely used in the 1950's by farmers to kill bugs that were destroying their crops. In the early 1960's DDT was found to be a harmful to wildlife, especially birds. DDT was banned in 1972 and is no longer used in the United States.

Diurnal   Animals that are active during the day.

Falconry   The art of training falcons and other birds of prey for hunting.

Juvenile   A bird that is young with feathers that are colored different than an adult bird. Most birds are juvenile until they turn one year old.

Mobbing   A behavior in which various bird species cooperatively attack or harass a raptor.

Molt   A bird molts when it loses its feathers, one by one, and a new feather grows in its place.

Nocturnal   Animals that are active at night.

Pesticide   A poison used to kill insects, weeds, or other pests.

Talons   Sharp claws of a raptor

Gallery of Raptors

With the exception of the vultures all the birds here are considered raptors. Some are highly specialized on their diet such as the snail kite which only eat snails.

Crested Caracara

Great Horned Owl

Bald Eagle

Northern Harrier

Sharp-shinned Hawk

Turkey Vulture

Barred Owl

Osprey

American Kestrel

Cooper's Hawk

Black Vulture

Barn Owl

Red-tailed Hawk

Merlin

Swallow-tailed Kite

Long-eared Owl

Eastern Screech Owl

Red-shouldered Hawk

Aplomado Falcon

Snail Kite

Ferruginous Pigmy Owl

Burrowing Owl

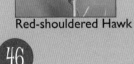

About the Raptor Project

The Raptor Project leads the way in wildlife education, bringing exciting educational programs and flight shows up close and personal to people throughout the United States. The Raptor Project is not a typical rehab center as most people are familiar with, but travels with 15 to 20 trained, live birds of prey (eagles, hawks, owls, and falcons) bringing their show to theme parks, fairs, festivals, schools, and many other venues across America.

The Raptor Project breeds many species of raptors and has perfected the raising, taming and training of raptors for spectacular educational shows. Many of their hand raised birds are featured in movies and commercials, working through animal acting agencies. Some are working for other bird shows at Disney World and Six Flags, as well as zoos and wildlife centers.

Raptor Project founders, Jonathan and Susan Wood, also adopt permanently handicapped birds from overcrowded wildlife centers to be part of their raptor presentations. Although these birds are not able to survive in the wild, they have become beloved ambassadors of their species to people young and old.

Jonathan Wood began working with birds of prey at only 12 years old and has always had a great passion for raptors. Starting the Raptor Project has allowed him to turn his hobby into his career. Along with his wife, Susan, and their daughter Rachel, they travel together as a family bringing the beauty and majesty of the magnificent raptors into the hearts of all who see their show.

Jonathan Wood holding a Golden Eagle during a performance.

Special Thanks...

A very special thanks to our gifted and talented friend & colleague, Reinier Munguia (Wildstock Photography), whose layout design has brought the words of this book to life. As a wildlife photographer, Reinier has also contributed many of the lovely photographs in these pages.

My husband, Jonathan Wood, has always encouraged me in all of my endeavors & provided helpful insight for Raptor Basics for Kids. Most of the photographs in this book are provided by Jonathan and Reinier, both gifted photographers.

I also would like to thank Jane Kirkland (Take a Walk Books) who has been an encouragement and guide for writing books.

Made in the USA
Charleston, SC
06 June 2014